DINOSAUR
SKELETONS
AND OTHER PREHISTORIC ANIMALS

A Reader's Digest Kids Book

Published by The Reader's Digest Association, Inc.

Conceived, edited, and designed by
Marshall Editions, London

Library of Congress Cataloging in Publication Data

Johnson, Jinny.
 Dinosaur skeletons and other prehistoric animals / written by
Jinny Johnson ; illustrated by Elizabeth Gray and Steve Kirk.
   p.   cm.
  ISBN 0-89577-678-2
  1. Dinosaurs—Juvenile literature.   [1. Dinosaurs.] I. Gray,
Elizabeth, 1969– ill. II. Kirk, Steve, ill.   III. Title.
QE862.D5J64 1995
567.9'1—dc20   94-35362
                                                      CIP
                                                      AC

Consultant: Dr. Barry Cox
Editors: Cynthia O'Brien, Kate Phelps
Designers: Branka Surla, Ralph Pitchford
Cover designer: Mike Harnden
Researcher: Liz Ferguson

The editors would like to thank the British
Museum (Natural History), London, and the
Royal Tyrrell Museum of Palaeontology,
Drumheller, Canada. The artist Elizabeth Gray
would like to thank Sandra Chapman at the
British Museum and Don Brinkman at the
Royal Tyrrell Museum for their help in the
making of this book.

Printed in EU Officine Grafiche De Agostini - Novara 1995
Bound by Legatoria del Verbano S.p.A.

DINOSAUR
SKELETONS
AND OTHER PREHISTORIC ANIMALS

Written by
Jinny Johnson

Illustrated by
Elizabeth Gray *and* **Steve Kirk**

READER'S DIGEST
Kids®

New York • Montreal

CONTENTS

Dinosaurs disappeared from the earth more than 60 million years before the first humans lived. But modern scientists have at least two ways of finding out about these great reptiles.

The first is by studying the fossilized bones, teeth, and other remains, such as footprints and eggs, that have been found. Teeth, for example, show what kinds of food the dinosaurs ate—sharp teeth belonged to meat eaters while plant eaters had blunter teeth. Marks on the bones where muscles were attached help experts to determine the size and shape of those muscles and to reconstruct the shape of the body. Fossil trackways, together with the proportions of leg bones, give an idea of how fast dinosaurs moved and whether they traveled in herds.

Dinosaurs had to cope with the same problems as modern animals—finding food, defending themselves, and looking after their young. Therefore, a second way of finding out about them is to compare them with similar animals living today. For example, *Gallimimus* looked similar to the ostrich and so, like the bird, was probably a fast runner.

There were two groups of dinosaurs, each containing several families. Other reptiles that lived alongside the dinosaurs included plesiosaurs, ichthyosaurs, and pterosaurs. The earliest known bird, *Archaeopteryx*, also lived at the same time as these prehistoric animals.

The names of these creatures are made up of Latin or Greek words that describe something about their appearance or behavior. The word *dinosaur* comes from the Greek for "terrible lizard." Here's how to say the names of the animals in this book:

Ornitholestes: *Orn-ith-oh-LEST-eez*
Gallimimus: *Gal-lee-MY-mus*
Dromaeosaurus: *Dro-may-oh-SORE-us*
Tyrannosaurus: *Tie-RAN-oh-sore-us*
Camarasaurus: *KAM-ah-rah-sore-us*
Diplodocus: *Dih-PLOD-uh-kus*
Iguanodon: *Ig-WAN-oh-don*
Lambeosaurus: *LAM-bee-oh-sore-us*
Stegoceras: *Steg-OSS-er-as*
Stegosaurus: *STEG-oh-sore-us*
Euoplocephalus: *Yoo-op-loh-SEF-ah-lus*
Triceratops: *Try-SER-rah-tops*
Ichthyosaurs: *IK-thee-oh-sores*
Plesiosaurs: *PLEE-zee-oh-sores*
Pterosaurs: *TER-oh-sores*
Archaeopteryx: *Ar-kee-OP-ter-ix*

ORNITHOLESTES

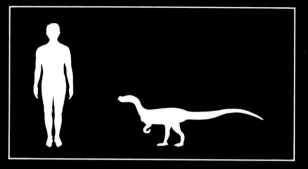

A small, lightly built dinosaur with a whiplike tail, *Ornitholestes* was a fast-moving hunter that caught prey in its slender, clawed hands. The pictures across the top here show how *Ornitholestes* chased and caught creatures such as lizards and frogs. It may also have scavenged food from the kills of larger dinosaurs.

Ornitholestes belonged to the coelurosaur group of dinosaurs, which were lightweight hunters. The name *coelurosaur* means "hollow-tailed lizard." It refers to the thin-walled, hollow bones that made up the tails of these dinosaurs and much of their slender bodies. *Ornitholestes* looked birdlike, and many scientists think birds may have evolved from dinosaurs similar to this one.

▲ *Ornitholestes* was only six feet long from nose to tail tip. It weighed 28 pounds—about the weight of a small dog.

Ornitholestes *had a larger, heavier skull than other coelurosaurs. Sharp teeth lined its strong jaws.*

On each hand Ornitholestes *had two very long fingers and one shorter finger. Claws on the fingers helped the dinosaur grasp its prey.*

Ornitholestes *walked upright on its back legs, leaving its slender front limbs free for grasping prey.*

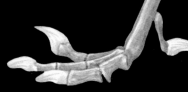

Scientists once thought that **Ornitholestes** *dragged its tail along the ground. Now most scientists believe that the dinosaur held its tail high to balance the front of the body as it ran.*

The long, slender tail of **Ornitholestes** *made up more than half its length.*

SPEEDY HUNTER

Western North America was the home of *Ornitholestes*. This swift hunter lived about 156 to 144 million years ago during the late Jurassic period. Its name means "bird robber," and it may have preyed on early birds or flying insects as well as reptiles.

The structure of the back legs shows that **Ornitholestes** *was a fast runner. The bones were light, and the ankle and toe bones long and slender.*

GALLIMIMUS

When running, Gallimimus held its long tail straight out. This helped balance its head and neck. (See the pictures in the top panel.)

Gallimimus moved upright on its two long back legs. Its feet, with their long upper bones and three slim toes, were ideally suited for running.

Fast-running *Gallimimus* was the largest of a group of dinosaurs known as ornithomimids, or "ostrich dinosaurs." With their slender legs, long, slim necks, and small heads, they looked like the ostriches of today, which are also swift runners.

Ornithomimids lived in Asia and North America and were intelligent, keen-sighted hunters. Scientists believe that the fastest "ostrich dinosaurs" could sprint at up to 40 miles an hour. In groups, they sped across open plains searching for prey. They also dug into the ground to find and eat eggs buried by other dinosaurs.

Speed was the ornithomimids' best defense in the face of danger. They did not have strong teeth or big claws to protect themselves from larger attackers, but few other dinosaurs could catch them when running at full speed.

10

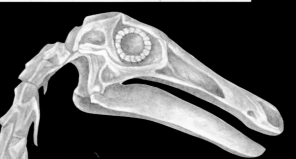

The long, flexible neck of **Gallimimus** supported a small, light head. Its long, narrow jaws gave this dinosaur a birdlike look. Because it had no teeth, **Gallimimus** swallowed its food whole.

Look at the big eye sockets. These held the large eyes that helped **Gallimimus** to spot prey—and danger. The ring of bony plates within the eye socket helped keep the shape of the eye.

Gallimimus *had slender hands, each with three sharp claws. It used these claws to capture and hold on to prey.*

▼ Nearly 17 feet long, *Gallimimus* was almost twice the size of a modern ostrich. The dinosaur weighed about 340 pounds— more than two adult people.

FAST MOVER

About 70 million years ago, *Gallimimus* lived in eastern Asia, in what is now Mongolia. This late Cretaceous dinosaur caught and ate insects and other small creatures such as lizards and frogs. It also pulled down the branches of trees with its long, clawed fingers and fed on leaves, buds, and fruits.

DROMAEOSAURUS

One of the fiercest hunters of its time, *Dromaeosaurus* was a slender, agile, two-legged dinosaur, built for fast movement. Many scientists believe that *Dromaeosaurus*, when running on two legs, could have reached a speed of almost 40 miles an hour. *Dromaeosaurus* lived in North America and belonged to the dromaeosaurid family. Other members of the family lived in Europe and Asia.

Dromaeosaurus was no larger than many other hunting dinosaurs of the time, but it had a special weapon—a large claw on the second toe of each foot. When hunting, the dinosaur chased its prey, then leapt off the ground to tear at the victim with these claws. (Look at the pictures at the top of the page to see *Dromaeosaurus* in action.)

The long tail was strengthened by bony rods growing backward from each of the tail bones. Muscles attached to these bony rods kept the tail stiff and still. This tail helped balance the dinosaur's body as it ran or attacked prey.

SPEEDY HUNTER

Dromaeosaurus lived in the late Cretaceous period, 76 to 70 million years ago. It had a large brain and was intelligent. Hunting in packs, dromaeosaurs could attack and bring down huge, plant-eating dinosaurs much larger than themselves.

This powerful hunter had a large head with strong jaws capable of delivering killing bites. Its teeth curved backward and had jagged edges for cutting into the thick skin of prey.

Each hand had three long fingers tipped with large, strong claws. *Dromaeosaurus* seized hold of prey with these hooklike hands.

Long, slender back legs helped make *Dromaeosaurus* a fast runner. Each foot had four toes. When running, *Dromaeosaurus* held the large, curved claws of the second toes off the ground.

▼ From its nose to the tip of its long tail, *Dromaeosaurus* was nearly six feet long. It weighed about 100 pounds.

TYRANNOSAURUS

Massive and ferocious, *Tyrannosaurus* is the biggest hunting animal known to have lived on land. It was the largest of the carnosaurs—the big, flesh-eating dinosaurs of the Jurassic and Cretaceous periods. All carnosaurs were bulky animals with powerful jaws and sharp teeth.

Tyrannosaurus walked upright on its two back legs and may have moved at 20 miles an hour or more. With its huge, heavy body, it could not chase prey for long. Instead, it stayed hidden among trees and waited for victims to come near. *Tyrannosaurus* then leapt out and charged toward its prey, killing it with fierce bites to the neck. Plant-eating dinosaurs such as *Edmontosaurus* and *Ankylosaurus* were probably its main food.

Tyrannosaurus also found food by scavenging—feeding on dead animals or taking prey from other predators.

Tyrannosaurus was about 40 feet long and 12 feet tall. When rearing up on its hind legs, this fierce meat-eating dinosaur reached 18 feet. It weighed six or seven tons—more than an African elephant today.

The skeleton of an animal as large as Tyrannosaurus had to be big enough to support its vast bulk but not so heavy that the animal could not move quickly enough to catch prey.

Like other dinosaurs that walked on two legs, Tyrannosaurus held its long tail straight out behind it. This helped balance the weight of the front part of its body, including its massive head.

The back leg bones were big and strong to support the heavy body. The ankle bones were fairly long, enabling it to move quickly over a short distance.

Each of the dinosaur's broad back feet had four toes—one small and three large toes, all with heavy claws.

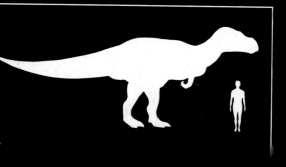

The massive skull of Tyrannosaurus *was nearly four feet long. Its jaws were three feet long and lined with 60 daggerlike teeth—some up to six inches in length. With these monstrous jaws and teeth, it could kill and rip apart prey in a matter of seconds.*

The arms and two-clawed hands of Tyrannosaurus *were surprisingly small for its huge body. They did not even reach to its mouth. Some experts think that the animal may have used its arms to lift itself off the ground after sleeping or feeding.*

Special ribs lined the belly of Tyrannosaurus. *They helped strengthen this part of the body.*

MIGHTY ATTACKER

This giant hunter lived in North America some 68 to 65 million years ago during the late Cretaceous period. With its large size, powerful jaws, and long, sharp teeth, *Tyrannosaurus* certainly deserved the name of "tyrant lizard."

CAMARASAURUS

Grooves in the tops of the neck and back vertebrae carried special long ligaments—bands of tough body tissue that hold bones together. These ligaments helped support the weight of the dinosaur's head and neck.

The skull of Camarasaurus was broad and deep, with large spaces to allow for the nostrils. These were high on the head—perhaps so they did not get blocked with leaves when the dinosaur fed. The jaws were studded with lots of chisel-shaped teeth, which the dinosaur used to strip leaves from branches.

There were twelve vertebrae in the long neck of Camarasaurus, compared to seven in the neck of a giraffe.

Large feet with five toes helped spread the massive weight of this dinosaur. The inside toe on each foot had a large, curved claw. The rest had blunt nails.

A plant-eating giant, mighty *Camarasaurus* belonged to the sauropod group of dinosaurs. Sauropods were the largest of all dinosaurs and the biggest land animals that have ever lived. All had huge bodies, thick, pillarlike legs, and long tails and necks. Most sauropods were more than 50 feet long. They were probably not fast movers and relied on their bulk to protect them from attack.

Animals of the size of *Camarasaurus* must have been extremely heavy. Some of the vertebrae and skull bones were hollow, making the skeleton lighter but just as strong.

Camarasaurus had a shorter neck than some other sauropods, such as *Diplodocus* (see pages 19–22), but could still reach up into trees to tear off mouthfuls of leaves. It moved on four legs and did not rear up on its back legs to feed. Just as crocodiles do today, *Camarasaurus* deliberately swallowed stones to help grind up the food in its stomach.

Huge ribs protected the deep body. The longest ribs were over six feet long—bigger than most adult humans. Five vertebrae were joined firmly to the massive hipbones, forming a solid support for the heavy body and tail.

▼ Nearly 60 feet in length, *Camarasaurus* was as long as a tractor trailer. It weighed 20 tons—more than three African elephants.

The special structure of its vertebrae (the bones that form the backbone) make **Diplodocus** light for its size. The vertebrae are partly hollow, so they weigh less than if they were made of solid bone.

The hipbones of **Diplodocus** had to be extremely strong to bear the weight of the body and tail. The five vertebrae above the hipbone were joined together to add more support.

The front feet of **Diplodocus** were broad and five-toed. The first toe of each foot probably had a large claw. These claws could have been used as weapons against attackers. The other toes ended in hooflike pads.

The legs of this dinosaur were like huge pillars supporting its long body. The back legs were longer than the front legs. The back feet had claws on the first and second toes.

DIPLODOCUS

O ne of the largest land animals that ever lived was *Diplodocus*. It belonged to the diplodocid family of long-necked dinosaurs, or sauropods, which also included the weighty *Apatosaurus*.

The sheer bulk of this peaceful plant eater protected it from most enemies. Only predators such as *Allosaurus*, the biggest meat-eating dinosaur of the time, would have been able to attack such a giant.

Diplodocus walked on four legs. It was not a fast mover. Its build and the footprints that have been found suggest that it walked at about the same speed as a human. Tracks also suggest that *Diplodocus* lived in herds as elephants do today. Young animals would have been protected by the adults in the herd (see the illustrations at the top of the page).

Vertebrae

The broad head of Diplodocus was small for such a giant animal. At just over two feet long, it was not much bigger than a horse's head. At the front of the mouth were rows of fine, closely packed teeth. The nostrils were right at the top of the head. In this position they were well out of the way of twigs and branches.

The neck of Diplodocus was about 24 feet long and contained 15 vertebrae.

◀ Although *Diplodocus* was more than 88 feet long—longer than a line of seven cars—it weighed only 11 tons, or slightly more than two African elephants. *Apatosaurus*, a relative of *Diplodocus*, was shorter but weighed about 30 tons.

Herd Dweller

Some 156 to 144 million years ago, in the late Jurassic period, groups of *Camarasaurus* roamed the moist tropical plains of western North America. These massive creatures moved in herds, which helped keep the young safe from attack by flesh-eating dinosaurs.

The tail of **Camarasaurus** *was short in comparison to that of other sauropods. It contained about 54 vertebrae, while some other sauropods had as many as 80. The V-shaped bones below the tail vertebrae protected blood vessels on the underside of the tail.*

IGUANODON

This dinosaur's long skull ended
in a powerful, toothless beak for
chopping off mouthfuls of plant
food. Farther back in the broad
snout were plenty of strong
teeth—useful for chewing tough
plants. New teeth developed as
old ones wore out.

A large, slow-moving plant
eater, *Iguanodon* was the
second dinosaur to be discovered.
Part of a leg bone was found in
England in 1809, and many more bones and
some teeth were found in 1822. When scientists
first put *Iguanodon* together, they placed the
dinosaur's thumb spike on its nose, believing it
to be a horn.

Iguanodon was a member of a family of heavily
built animals known as iguanodonts, which
lived all over the world. These dinosaurs could
walk on two legs but also moved on all four.

Fossil footprints show that *Iguanodon* traveled
in herds for safety. Smaller predators would not
have dared to attack a group of these mighty
creatures. Also, a threatened *Iguanodon* could
run at about 20 miles an hour on two legs or, if
need be, defend itself with its thumb spike.

On each hand Iguanodon
had a sharp spike instead of a
thumb. The animal used it to
jab at the eye or neck of an
attacker. The three middle
fingers were like pointed
hooves; Iguanodon used
these when it walked on all
fours. The fifth finger could
be bent across the palm and
used to grasp food.

23

PLANT-EATING GIANT

Diplodocus lived in western North America about 140 million years ago, during the late Jurassic period. A plant eater, its fine teeth would have been ideal for stripping leaves from plants but not for chewing. The discovery of smooth pebbles near the fossils of these dinosaurs suggests that sauropods swallowed stones to help grind up food inside their stomachs. Birds today swallow grit and small stones for the same reason.

The bones beneath the tail vertebrae helped protect the underside of the tail.

Bony tendons—slim rods of bone—crisscrossed the spines of Iguanodon's backbone. The tendons helped strengthen the backbone and support the heavy tail.

To support Iguanodon's bulk, leg bones were large and sturdy. Each foot had three strong toes, tipped with hooflike claws. Iguanodon walked on its toes.

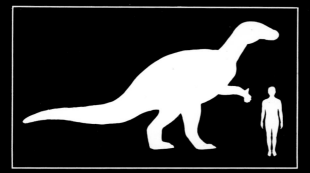

▲ Iguanodon was 33 feet long and 9 feet high at the hips. It weighed about 5 tons—as much as a modern African elephant.

The long tail of **Diplodocus** was made up of at least 70 vertebrae. Marks on the bones show that large muscles powered the tail, enabling the dinosaur to lash its whiplike end from side to side to fend off enemies.

When the first **Diplodocus** skeletons were put together, they showed the dinosaur with its tail dragging on the ground. But although many footprints of this type of dinosaur have been found, there are few signs of dragging tails. Experts now think that **Diplodocus** carried its tail up off the ground as it walked.

PEACEFUL PLANT EATER

Herds of *Iguanodon* roamed Europe during the early Cretaceous period, 128 to 108 million years ago. They browsed on such plants as ferns and horsetails growing along rivers and streams. An *Iguanodon* could also feed on tree foliage if it stood up on its two hind legs, using its long tail as a prop.

*A heavy tail held straight out behind the body helped balance **Iguanodon**'s weight when it walked on two legs.*

V-shaped bones below the tail protected the blood vessels that ran underneath the backbone.

25

LAMBEOSAURUS

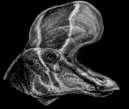

A large, sturdy plant eater, *Lambeosaurus* belonged to a group of dinosaurs called hadrosaurs. These dinosaurs are also known as duckbills because of their long, flattened, horn-covered beak.

Some hadrosaurs had flat heads. Others had oddly shaped crests on the tops of their heads. Different species had crests of different shapes, as you can see in the pictures at the top of the page. It is possible that the crests of males and females of the same species varied in shape and size.

Hollow passages inside the crest may have acted like echo chambers to make the hadrosaur's booming calls even louder. The shape of the crest affected the sound, so each kind of hadrosaur may have had its own call. Hadrosaurs lived in herds, and experts think that their crests and calls helped them to recognize and keep in touch with others of their own species as well as to find mates.

Lambeosaurus had two structures on its head—a tall, hollow crest and a solid, bony spike behind it.

The neck was strong yet flexible, allowing Lambeosaurus *to gather low-growing plants from a wide area without having to move too much.*

Like all hadrosaurs, Lambeosaurus *used its toothless beak to nip off plant food. It then chewed the food with the teeth farther back in its jaws.*

26

▲ *Lambeosaurus* measured about 33 feet from nose to tail—as long as three cars. It weighed as much as three tons.

When feeding, Lambeosaurus usually moved on four legs. When it needed to escape quickly from predators, it probably reared up on its back legs to run away. This skeleton of Lambeosaurus is shown crouched down in a drinking position.

The tail was large and heavy. It was held straight out to balance the body when Lambeosaurus walked on two legs.

GROUP NESTER

Lambeosaurus lived in North America some 76 million years ago during the late Cretaceous period. The remains of nests found together suggest that some types of hadrosaurs nested in groups. Each female scraped a hollow in the earth to make a safe pit for her eggs. Once hatched, the young dinosaurs probably stayed in the nesting colony while the parents found food to bring them.

STEGOCERAS

The top of the eight-inch-long skull was a high dome of solid bone. This took the force of the impact when Stegoceras crashed head on into a rival. The domes grew larger with age, and males had bigger domes than females.

The back vertebrae had special joints that held them tightly locked together and prevented them from twisting out of line during head-crashing battles. Thin, bony rods, or tendons, running between the vertebrae strengthened the back further.

The jaws of Stegoceras contained slightly curved, jagged-edged teeth. These were ideally shaped for tearing up plant food.

Special ribs lined the belly and helped strengthen this part of the body.

Although peaceful creatures for most of the time, male *Stegoceras* dinosaurs probably took part in fierce battles during the mating season. They charged toward one another with head lowered and neck, body, and tail held straight out (see pictures at the top of the page). The rivals clashed head on, and the thickened bony dome on their heads acted as a built-in crash helmet to protect them. Some experts think the beasts also rammed each other's sides.

Stegoceras belonged to a family of dinosaurs called pachycephalosaurs, which means "thick-headed lizards." The largest pachycephalosaurs had skulls capped with solid bone up to ten inches thick. Many also had bony frills and spikes around the dome.

Stegoceras *moved upright on its two back legs. Its arms were much shorter and were used to handle food.*

When held straight out, the heavy tail of this dinosaur helped balance the weight of its domed head.

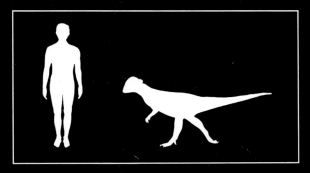

▲ From its head to the end of its tail, *Stegoceras* measured about six feet long.

DOMED DINOSAUR

S *tegoceras* lived in North America and China in the late Cretaceous period, 75 to 68 million years ago. Like all pachycephalosaurs, it fed on plants. The dome on the top of the head may have been brightly colored, as shown here.

STEGOSAURUS

One of the most easily recognized of all dinosaurs, *Stegosaurus* was the biggest of the group known as stegosaurs, or "plated dinosaurs." Typical of its kind, *Stegosaurus* was a large, slow-moving plant eater with a small head. Its huge body was topped with double rows of large, bony plates.

What was the purpose of these flattened bones? Many experts now think that they were a way of controlling body temperature. Blood-rich skin may have covered the plates. When a *Stegosaurus* was cold, it would turn its side toward the sun. The sun's heat would warm the blood as it passed over the plates on its way around the body. When facing away from the sun and into a breeze, the plates would give off heat and thus cool the animal.

The plates on the back of Stegosaurus *were probably arranged in two alternating rows, as shown here. People used to think they were arranged in pairs. The largest plates were two feet wide and two feet tall.*

Stegosaurus *had an extremely small skull for such a large animal. The skull was only about 16 inches long and protected a brain the size of a walnut.*

◀ At more than 24 feet long, *Stegosaurus* was longer than an African elephant and weighed as much as two tons.

PLANT EATER

Although *Stegosaurus* usually moved on four legs, it may have reared up on two legs to feed on the branches of trees, as shown here. *Stegosaurus* lived in western North America 156 to 144 million years ago during the late Jurassic period. Other kinds of stegosaurs lived in Europe, Africa, and China.

The massive back legs were more than twice as long as the front legs, so the body of Stegosaurus sloped forward from its highest point at the hips. The broad, three-toed feet helped spread the body's great weight. Short front legs allowed the head on its short neck to be brought down to the ground for feeding. The front feet had five strong, clawed toes.

At the end of the tail were foot-long spikes covered in tough horn, like the horns of cattle. Stegosaurus defended itself by lashing attackers with this spiked tail.

31

EUOPLOCEPHALUS

Studded with spikes and horns and armed with a tail ending in a bony club, *Euoplocephalus* was built like a tank and able to defend itself against most enemies. Its heavy body was covered with plates of bone set into its leathery skin, making it difficult to bite or attack. Even its eyelids were armored—pieces of bone came down like shutters over the normal lids to protect the eyes from sharp claws. A predator's only chance was to try and turn *Euoplocephalus* over onto its back—its undersides were less well protected than the rest of its body.

Euoplocephalus belonged to the ankylosaur, or "armored dinosaur," group. They were sturdy creatures with clublike tails. *Euoplocephalus* moved on four legs and fed on plants, nipping leaves off with the toothless beak at the front of its broad head.

The body, sides, and front legs of Euoplocephalus *were protected by rows of triangular spikes jutting out of the skin.*

Horn

Euoplocephalus *had an extremely strong skull, with a covering of extra pieces of bone. At the back of the skull were short, triangular horns giving more protection to the head.*

CLUB-TAILED DINOSAUR

E*uoplocephalus* lived in North America 80 to 70 million years ago during the late Cretaceous period. If attacked while it searched for food, this ankylosaur would lash out with its clublike tail. A blow from this bony weapon could injure even a large predator, such as *Tyrannosaurus*.

The club on the end of the tail was made up of two large balls of bone joined together. The bones of the tail were stiffened and strengthened with bony tendons—thin bony rods— to support the heavy club.

Heavy hipbones carried large powerful muscles. These helped Euoplocephalus swing its clubbed tail from side to side. The club weighed more than 60 pounds—as much as a seven-year-old child.

▼ Including its long tail, *Euoplocephalus* measured about 20 feet in length. It weighed about two tons.

Sturdy leg bones helped support the weight of this heavily armored dinosaur. Euoplocephalus was agile for its size and able to run away from danger.

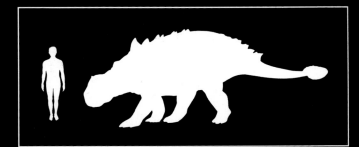

33

TRICERATOPS

Long, sharp horns and a bony frill around its neck kept *Triceratops* safe from the fiercest of enemies—even *Tyrannosaurus*. If threatened, this horned creature charged like a giant rhinoceros.

Triceratops was one of the largest of the group known as ceratopsians, or "horned dinosaurs." A large, heavy plant eater, it roamed the forests to find food. It was not a fast mover and did not rely on speed for defense.

Male *Triceratops* also used their sharp horns to battle for leadership of the herd and the chance to mate with females. Rival males locked horns and pushed against one another with their bony neck frills (shown in the pictures at the top of the page).

The neck frill was a solid sheet of bone. It acted as a protective shield for the neck and shoulders. The frill may have been brightly colored.

The huge skull of **Triceratops** *measured up to seven feet from the nose to the back of the head. The two horns on the brow were around three feet long, and the short horn on the nose measured about seven inches.*

At the front of the mouth was a sharp beak. **Triceratops** *used this to bite off mouthfuls of tough plants. The food was then chewed farther back in the jaws with its grinding teeth.*

34

◀ *Triceratops* was 30 feet long, 10 feet tall, and 9 tons in weight. Imagine an animal twice the length of a rhinoceros and heavier than a full-grown African elephant.

HORNED GIANT

Massive *Triceratops* wandered western North America 68 to 65 million years ago, during the late Cretaceous period. If threatened, it would use its massive horned head to ward off its attacker.

The long hipbones of Triceratops *were attached to a greater than normal number of vertebrae— the bones that make up the backbone. This made the body stronger.*

Triceratops *walked on four legs. The leg bones of this dinosaur were thick and strong to carry the weight of its huge body and head.*

On the feet were short, wide toes—five on the front feet and four on the back—fanned out to help spread the animal's weight. They were the feet of a plodder, not a fast runner.

ICHTHYOSAURS

Eye socket

*The skull ended in a long, slender snout. Unlike most other ichthyosaurs, **Ophthalmosaurus** appears to have had no teeth. Most likely it caught prey in its beaklike jaws and swallowed it whole.*

The limbs of ichthyosaurs were shaped like paddles and were used for steering as they swam. The large front paddles were supported by extra bones.

While dinosaurs roamed the land, such sea-living reptiles as ichthyosaurs ruled the open waters. The name *ichthyosaur* means "fish lizard"; these reptiles look like fish because of their streamlined bodies and fishlike tails. The biggest ichthyosaur ever found was 50 feet long, but most measured only 6 to 12 feet long.

For about 100 million years, ichthyosaurs, such as *Ophthalmosaurus,* cruised the seas of the world. They lived much like today's dolphins, which are air-breathing mammals. Fast and agile, they could speed through the sea at up to 25 miles an hour. They hunted such prey as fish, squid, and the now-extinct squidlike belemnites. They also gave birth to their young in water.

Although they lived in the sea, ichthyosaurs were reptiles and had to come to the surface to breathe air. Their nostrils were set high up on the skull. This meant that the animals did not have to poke their heads far out of the water to breathe.

Ophthalmosaurus *had particularly large eyes, which may have helped it hunt at night. A bony ring surrounded each eye. This maintained the shape of the eyeball when the ichthyosaur was swimming in the deep sea where water pressure is high.*

▲ The sleek and graceful body of *Ophthalmosaurus* was 11 feet long—about the length of a small car. It had a large, powerful tail.

The end of the backbone bent sharply down to support the lower part of the large tail. The tail provided the main swimming power for ichthyosaurs.

OCEAN DWELLER

Ophthalmosaurus lived in the late Jurassic period, 160 to 157 million years ago. Unlike most reptiles, ichthyosaurs did not lay eggs but gave birth to live young. Like dolphins today, the babies were born tail first. A fossil found in Germany shows an ichthyosaur giving birth in this way.

37

PLESIOSAURS

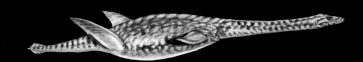

Plesiosaurs were reptiles that lived in the sea at the same time that dinosaurs walked the earth. They were well adapted to aquatic life. Many kinds of plesiosaurs, such as *Cryptoclidus*, had small heads, long necks, and four paddle-shaped flippers. Like sea turtles today, they beat these flippers up and down in slow, steady movements to push themselves along in the water (see the pictures in the top panel).

Plesiosaurs spent nearly all their lives at sea, but they came to land to lay eggs. Like turtles, they dragged themselves up onto a beach and laid their eggs in pits that they made in the sand. When the young hatched, they made their own way down to the sea.

▲ Nose to tail, *Cryptoclidus* measured as much as 13 feet— longer than an average car. Some plesiosaurs were much larger—up to 46 feet long.

Belly ribs joined the shoulder bones and hipbones and made the plesiosaur's short body stronger and more rigid. This helped make a solid structure to support the powerful movements of the flippers.

Belly ribs

Cryptoclidus had long, narrow flippers instead of legs. In each toe, there were as many as ten bones. They helped make the flippers flexible.

The skull of Cryptoclidus *was small in relation to the body. It had a broad, flat snout, and its jaws held many sharp, curved teeth.*

When feeding, the plesiosaur opened its mouth, taking in water and lots of small fish and shrimp. When it closed its jaws again, the teeth formed a sieve, allowing water to drain out, while the food stayed inside the mouth.

The shoulder bones and hipbones were large and flat. Powerful muscles connected to these bones moved the flippers.

LONG-NECKED HUNTER

Cryptoclidus lived in European seas during the late Jurassic period, or about 135 million years ago. *Cryptoclidus* could stretch out its neck to catch passing prey and also raise its head above water to look for food. That long neck, however, also made *Cryptoclidus* an easy target for bigger predators.

39

PTEROSAURS

When dinosaurs lived on land, flying reptiles called pterosaurs ruled the skies. As far as scientists know, pterosaurs were the first vertebrates—animals with backbones—to fly. They had wings made of skin attached to an extra long finger on each hand.

Pterosaurs ranged in size from small species about the size of a blackbird to the largest flying creatures ever. The biggest pterosaur was probably *Quetzalcoatlus*, which measured 40 feet from wing tip to wing tip—about the same wingspan as a light airplane's.

There were two kinds of pterosaurs. The earliest forms, called rhamphorhynchoids, had short legs and long, bony tails. Later came the pterodactyls, such as *Anhanguera*, which had short tails and longer necks and legs. Pterosaurs became extinct at the same time as the dinosaurs— about 64 million years ago.

Like all pterosaurs, Anhanguera had an extremely light skeleton. Its bones were slender and many were hollow which made them even lighter.

Anhanguera's skull was nearly twice as long as its tiny body. On the top jaw was a crest that helped steady the head when the pterosaur plunged its jaws into water to catch fish.

The first three fingers of Anhanguera's hand were short and tipped with sharp claws. The fourth finger was extremely long and supported the top edge of the wing. The wing was also attached to the side of the body, possibly at about hip level.

▼ The pterosaur *Anhanguera* measured 13 feet from wing tip to wing tip. It was bigger than a wandering albatross, the bird with the longest wings today, which has a wingspan of up to 11 feet. Although its wings were large, the body of this pterosaur was only 9–10 inches long.

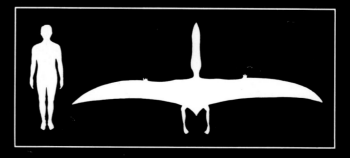

Pteroid

A special bone near the wrist joint, called the pteroid, was joined to the upper wing. This part of the wing stretched between the pterosaur's neck and arm. The pteroid may have helped control the upper wing.

On each foot were five toes. Four were long and tipped with claws. The fifth was short and did not have a claw.

Experts disagree about how Anhanguera moved on the ground. Some believe that it walked upright on its two back feet like a modern bird. Others say that the structure of its hipbones shows that it could not have stood upright. They think that it crawled along using the claws on its front wings as well as its feet.

FISH EATER

A nhanguera lived in northern South America about 120 to 110 million years ago, during the late Cretaceous period. It probably fed on fish that it seized from the water. Its long, slender jaws and sharp teeth were ideally shaped for grasping slippery fish.

41

ARCHAEOPTERYX

The earliest known bird, *Archaeopteryx*, was an extraordinary link between birds and reptiles such as dinosaurs. It had features of both groups. Like reptiles, *Archaeopteryx* had toothed jaws, a long, bony tail, and clawed fingers. Like birds, it had feathers on its wings and tail.

The first *Archaeopteryx* skeletons were found in 1861 in southern Germany. The detail of the fossil skeletons was so fine that an impression of feathers could be seen, proving that these creatures were not just small dinosaurs. The fossils showed that *Archaeopteryx* had wings just like those of birds today, and suggested that it would have been able to fly. But *Archaeopteryx* did not have the large breastbone of modern birds, which supports powerful flapping muscles. As a result, it probably could not flap up into the air from the ground but, instead, had to launch itself into the air from an elevated position such as the branch of a tree.

▲ *Archaeopteryx* was 14 inches long from head to tail—about the same size as a crow today.

TREE CLIMBER

Archaeopteryx lived in Europe about 150 million years ago, during the late Jurassic period. It fed on insects, flapping and gliding through the air in search of its prey. But *Archaeopteryx* could only fly for short periods and would have had to land on the ground. It would then have used its claws to climb up into trees in order to jump off into the air and fly again.

42

The skull was long, narrow, and birdlike. **Archaeopteryx** had small, sharp teeth in its jaws, unlike modern birds, which do not have teeth.

On each of the long arms of **Archaeopteryx** was a three-clawed hand. The claws projected from the edge of the wing. Large feathers transformed the arms and hands into wings.

Like most dinosaurs, **Archaeopteryx** had a long, bony tail, but fossils show that it was fringed by feathers. These would have helped the bird glide through the air. Some modern birds have long tail feathers, but their bony tail is short.

Like modern birds, **Archaeopteryx** had a wishbone formed from its collarbones. The wishbone supported some of the muscles used for flapping the wings.

The legs of **Archaeopteryx** were long and slim. On each foot were four toes. Three toes pointed forward and one backward—the same arrangement most birds have today.

TIME LINE

KEY
Ocean
Land
Shallow sea

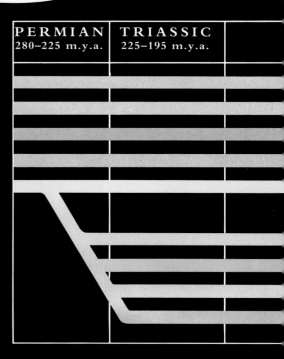

In the Triassic period much of the world's land was joined together. This supercontinent was known as Pangaea.

Dinosaurs and other reptiles such as plesiosaurs, pterosaurs, and ichthyosaurs dominated life on earth for more than 140 million years, from the late Triassic to the end of the Cretaceous.

The top chart here shows the dinosaurs in relation to other types of animals. It shows, for example, how birds are believed to be related to dinosaurs. The lower chart shows the two groups of dinosaurs in more detail and the links among the dinosaurs shown in this book.

At the time of the dinosaurs, the world did not look as it does now. The continents, once all joined in one land mass, were slowly drifting apart. The maps at the top of the page show the changing shape of the dinosaurs' world.

PERMIAN 280–225 m.y.a.	TRIASSIC 225–195 m.y.a.	

Note: m.y.a. means "million years ago."

TRIASSIC
225–195 m.y.a.

SAURISCHIANS

ORNITHISCHIANS

JURASSIC
195–135 m.y.a.

IGUANODONTS–Iguanodon, p. 23

HADROSAURS–Lambeosaurus, p. 26

CERATOPSIANS–Triceratops, p. 34

PACHYCEPHALOSAURS–Stegoceras, p. 28

STEGOSAURS–Stegosaurus, p. 30

ANKYLOSAURS–Euoplocephalus, p. 32

SAUROPODS–Camarasaurus, p. 16; Diplodocus, p. 19

COELUROSAURS–Ornitholestes, p. 8

DROMAEOSAURS–Dromaeosaurus, p. 12

ORNITHOMIMIDS–Gallimimus, p. 10

CARNOSAURS–Tyrannosaurus, p. 14

In the early Cretaceous period North America split from South America and a sea separated Europe from Asia.

By the late Cretaceous period continents had drifted farther apart. North America was divided in two by a sea.

SSIC m.y.a.	CRETACEOUS 135–64 m.y.a.	CENOZOIC 64 m.y.a.–present day
		TORTOISES/TURTLES
		MAMMALS
ICHTHYOSAURS–Ophthalmosaurus, p.36		
PLESIOSAURS–Cryptoclidus, p.38		
		LIZARDS
		SNAKES
		CROCODILES
	PTEROSAURS–Anhanguera, p.40	
	ORNITHISCHIAN DINOSAURS	} SEE DETAILED CHART BELOW
	SAURISCHIAN DINOSAURS	
BIRDS–Archaeopteryx p.42		

At the end of the Cretaceous period, 64 million years ago, all dinosaurs, ichthyosaurs, plesiosaurs, and pterosaurs had died out. No one knows why this extraordinary mass extinction occurred, but many experts think that a giant meteorite hit the earth at this time. The huge amount of rock thrown into the atmosphere by the impact would have changed the earth's climate for many years. Some types of animals, such as dinosaurs, would have been unable to survive this change.

e animals on the charts are those
ured in this book. The darker
red areas on the bars show the
iod during which each type of
mal probably existed.

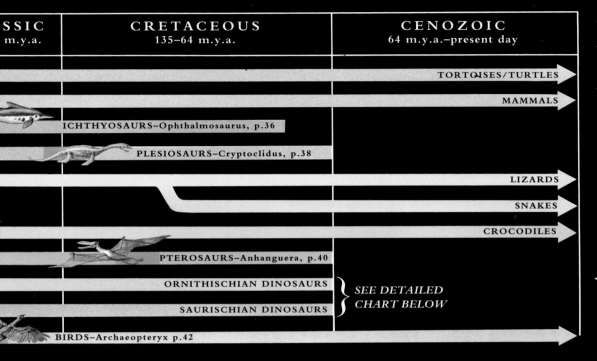

CRETACEOUS
135–64 m.y.a.

Both groups of dinosaurs included several families. Each family contained many different types of osaurs. For example, the hadrosaur ily in the ornithischian group luded the dinosaur *Lambeosaurus* about 16 other known species.

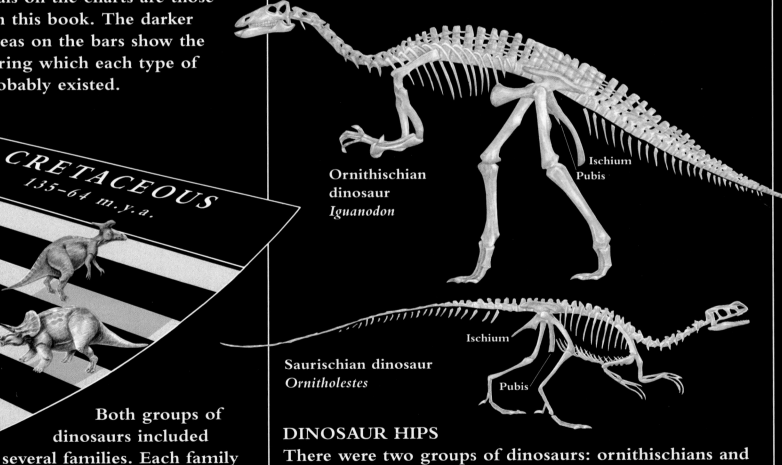

Ornithischian dinosaur *Iguanodon*

Ischium
Pubis

Saurischian dinosaur *Ornitholestes*

Ischium
Pubis

DINOSAUR HIPS
There were two groups of dinosaurs: ornithischians and saurischians. The main differences between them lay in the hipbones. In saurischians, the pubis bone points away from the ischium bone. In ornithischians, part of the pubis runs below the ischium (see pictures).

45

INDEX